contents

Introduction

contents

introduction

Vegetarian eating is a healthy alternative for today's lifestyle. Meals without meat, poultry or seafood are attractive, tasty and satisfying – as well as being good for you. The recipes in this book provide delectable dishes which can be combined, or can be enjoyed as a hearty meal on their own. Influenced by cuisines from around the world, there are easy-to-prepare dishes which have the wonderful texture and flavour of fresh vegetables, raw and cooked.

From an Asian-influenced soup to scrumptious desserts, this selection of satisfying and delicious recipes will enable you to prepare natural healthy food to suit every appetite and for every occasion, from a quick snack to a three-course dinner party.

Good for you

Health authorities recommend that we eat four serves of vegetables daily, at least one of which should be raw. The old adage of a white, a yellow and a green may be rarely taught these days, but it is a good reminder that the brightly coloured vegetables are usually the best source of vitamins. Most of the vitamin content lies just under the skin, so vegetables should be cooked and eaten with the skin on as often as possible.

To make the most of your garden-fresh vegetables, we have put together these essential step-by-step preparation and cooking tips to help you create your own.

Easy cooking and preparation depends on having a few good basic pieces of equipment. To make life easier for you, it is worth investing a little time and money in some good equipment such as a large chopping board, a small sharp vegetable or paring knife, as well as several larger sharp knives for cutting and chopping, a grater, a vegetable peeler and a colander or large sieve. Remember to keep your knives sharp: either learn to sharpen them yourself or take them to a knife sharpener regularly. Sharp knives make preparation a breeze.

Wash vegetables before preparing, but do not soak. Soaking tends to draw out the valuable water-soluble vitamins and you end up with vegetables with a lower nutrient content. As with every rule there are always exceptions and it may be necessary to soak very dirty vegetables to remove dirt and creepy-crawlies. If this is the case, always keep soaking times to a minimum.

- Vegetables that are left whole with their skins on have a higher nutrient and fibre content than those that are finely chopped and peeled. Many of the precious vitamins and minerals found in vegetables are stored just under the skin. Only peel vegetables if necessary.

- For maximum nutritional value, prepare vegetables just before cooking and serve as soon as they are cooked.

- The smaller the portion, the quicker the cooking time. For example, grated carrot will cook more quickly than carrot cut into slices.

soups
& starters

coconut,
sweet potato

and spinach soup

30g/1oz butter
455g/16oz sweet potatoes, cut into 1cm/^{1}/$_2$in dice
1 onion, chopped
2 cloves garlic, crushed
1 tsp grated fresh root ginger
1 tbsp medium curry paste
600mL/21oz vegetable stock
200mL/7fl oz/ coconut milk
juice of 1 lime
^{1}/$_4$ tsp dried crushed chillies
170g/6oz fresh spinach, shredded
salt and black pepper

1 Melt the butter in a saucepan and fry the potatoes, onion, garlic, ginger and curry paste for 5 minutes or until lightly golden.

2 Add the stock, coconut milk, lime juice and chilli. Bring to the boil, cover and simmer for 15 minutes or until the potatoes are tender.

3 Leave the soup to cool a little, then purée half of it with a hand blender. Return the purée to the pan, add the spinach and cook for 1-2 minutes, until the spinach has just wilted and the soup has heated through. Season to taste.

Note: Sweet potatoes have a slightly nutty flavour. They also make the texture of this coconut soup really creamy. For a fantastic light meal, serve the soup with naan bread.

vine

tomatoes and goat's cheese bruschetta

455g/16oz small vine-ripened tomatoes

2 tbsp extra virgin olive oil

1 clove garlic, crushed

4 sprigs fresh thyme

4 thick slices ciabatta, cut on the diagonal

4 tbsp ready-made tapenade

100g/3^1/$_2$oz soft goat's cheese, cut into chunks

fresh basil leaves to garnish

1 Preheat the oven to 220°C/425°F/Gas Mark 7. Place the tomatoes, still on the vine, in a roasting tin and drizzle over the oil. Scatter over the garlic and thyme sprigs. Roast for 15 minutes or until the tomatoes are tender. Divide the tomatoes into 4 portions of roughly the same size, each still attached to part of the vine.

2 Meanwhile, preheat the grill to high. Toast the bread on both sides until golden. Spread each slice with 1 tablespoon of tapenade, add a few chunks of goat's cheese and top with the tomatoes on the vine. Drizzle over the juices from the roasting tin and sprinkle with the basil leaves.

Serves *4* ***Preparation*** *10mins* ***Cooking*** *15mins* ***Calories*** *278* ***Fat*** *23g*

pea

and fresh mint soup

55g/2oz butter

2 rashers rindless streaky bacon, chopped

bunch of spring onions, chopped

455g/16oz shelled fresh peas, or frozen peas

2 mignonette lettuces, shredded

salt and black pepper

2 tbsp chopped fresh mint

145mL/5oz carton single cream

pinch of superfine sugar (optional)

fresh lemon juice (optional)

single cream to serve and snipped fresh chives to garnish

1 Melt the butter in a large heavy-based saucepan, add the bacon and cook for 2-3 minutes, then add the spring onions. Cover and cook gently for 5 minutes, stirring once or twice, until the onions have softened but not browned.

2 Add the peas and lettuce and 900mL/32fl oz of water. Season well, bring to the boil, then simmer for 10 minutes or until the vegetables are tender. Purée with the mint and cream until smooth, using a food processor or a hand blender.

3 Return the soup to the pan. Season again, if necessary, then add the superfine sugar and lemon juice, if using. Reheat gently but do not allow the soup to boil. Serve in bowls with a spoonful of cream drizzled over and a sprinkling of chives.

Serves 4   *Preparation* 15mins   *Cooking* 25mins   *Calories* 335   *Fat* 25g

sweet
pepper terrine

1 Preheat the oven to 190°C/375°F/Gas Mark 5. Butter a large piece of baking paper and line a 455g/16oz loaf tin, leaving enough paper to cover the top. Finely dice half a red and half a yellow pepper (capsicum) and set aside. Roughly chop the rest.

2 Heat the oil in a heavy-based saucepan, add the chopped peppers (capsicum) and chilli, then cook, covered, for 20 minutes or until softened. Purée in a food processor or with a hand blender, then press through a sieve. Combine the ricotta, Cheddar, mustard, salt and eggs, then stir in the purée and diced peppers (capsicum). Pour into the tin, then fold the paper over to cover the terrine without touching. Place in a roasting tin.

3 Pour in enough boiling water to reach halfway up the sides of the loaf tin, then cook for 1 hour 15 minutes, adding more water if necessary. Cool for 2 hours, then place in the fridge for 1 hour. Invert onto a plate and peel off the paper. To make the vinaigrette, combine the ingredients, mixing well. Serve the terrine in slices with the vinaigrette.

butter for greasing

2 red and 2 yellow peppers (capsicum), halved and deseeded

3 tbsp olive oil

1 red chilli, deseeded and thinly sliced

255g/9oz tub ricotta

115g/4oz mature Cheddar, grated

1 tbsp Dijon mustard

1 tsp salt

3 medium eggs, beaten

For the vinaigrette

2 tbsp white wine vinegar

2 tbsp extra virgin olive oil

4 tbsp sunflower oil

2 spring onions, finely sliced

3 tbsp finely chopped fresh basil

salt and black pepper

Serves 6   **Preparation** 25mins plus 2hrs cooling and 1hr chilling
Cooking 1hr 35mins   **Calories** 1439   **Fat** 40g

vegetable oil for greasing

1 tbsp freshly grated Parmesan

85g/3oz watercress, finely chopped, thick stems discarded

4 medium eggs, beaten

salt and black pepper

For the filling

200g/7oz full-fat soft cheese, at room temperature

3 tbsp full-fat milk

85g/3oz watercress, finely chopped and thick stems discarded, with a few sprigs reserved to garnish

5 spring onions, finely chopped

Serves *4* ***Preparation*** *20mins plus 40mins cooling and 30mins chilling*
Cooking *8mins* ***Calories*** *266* ***Fat*** *23g*

watercress
roulade with parmesan

1 Preheat the oven to 200°C/400°F/Gas Mark 6. Grease a 23 x 30cm/9 x 12in swiss roll tin, line with baking paper, then sprinkle with ½ tablespoon of Parmesan.

2 Mix together the watercress and eggs, season, then pour into the tin. Cook for 7-8 minutes, until the eggs have set. Remove from the oven and leave to cool for 5 minutes. Sprinkle over the remaining Parmesan. Lay a sheet of baking paper over the top and set aside for 35 minutes or until completely cool.

3 To make the filling, mix the cream cheese with the milk, watercress, onions and seasoning. Turn the cooled roulade onto a chopping board. Peel off the top sheet of paper, then spread the filling over the base. Roll up from the short end, peeling off the paper as you go. Refrigerate for 30 minutes, then serve in slices, garnished with watercress.

red onion and chilli tarts

370g/13oz pack ready-rolled puff pastry

1 tbsp olive oil

200g/7oz red onions, halved and finely sliced lengthways

1 small red chilli, deseeded and thinly sliced

salt and black pepper

2 tbsp red pesto

30g/1oz pine nut kernels

1 Preheat the oven to 220°C/425°F/Gas Mark 7. Open out the pastry sheet and cut out 4 x 12cm/4½in rounds. Use a slightly smaller cutter or a sharp knife to score a 1cm/½in border on each – this will form the rim. Place the rounds on a baking sheet.

2 Heat the oil in a large frying pan. Fry the onions for 10 minutes or until softened, stirring. Add the chilli and cook gently for 1 minute, then season.

3 Spread the pesto over the pastry rounds, leaving the rim clear. Spoon the onion mixture over the pesto and scatter over the pine nut kernels. Cook for 12-15 minutes, until the pastry has risen and is golden brown.

***Serves** 4   **Preparation** 15mins   **Cooking** 25mins   **Calories** 477   **Fat** 33g*

vegetable

bhajis

10 shallots, finely chopped

2 courgettes (zucchini), coarsely grated

1 aubergine (eggplant), finely diced

vegetable oil for frying

For the batter

100g/3 $^{1}/_{2}$oz gram (chickpea) flour

55g/2oz ground rice

$^{1}/_{4}$ tsp baking soda

1 tsp chilli powder

1 tsp turmeric

1-2 tbsp curry powder (mild or hot according to taste)

1 tsp salt

Serves 4
Preparation 25mins
Cooking 30mins
Calories 52
Fat 20g

1 To make the batter, put all the ingredients into a bowl, then gradually add 225mL/8fl oz of water, stirring constantly until combined. Add the shallots, courgettes (zucchini) and aubergine (eggplant) to the batter, mixing well.

2 Pour the oil into a wok to a depth of 5cm/2in and heat over a medium to high heat. Check the oil is hot enough by dropping in a small piece of vegetable; it should sizzle. Gently place 4 balls of the mixture (about 2 tablespoons each) into the hot oil and fry for 2-3 minutes, until golden. Turn over and cook for a further 2-3 minutes, until crisp.

3 Remove the bhajis with a slotted spoon and drain on kitchen towels. Fry the remaining bhajis in the same way.

2

fresh
salads

lettuce,

avocado & peanut salad

2 mignonette lettuces, leaves separated

1 head chicory, leaves separated

2 small ripe avocados, stoned, peeled and cut into chunks

3 spring onions, chopped

3 tbsp salted peanuts

For the dressing

1 tbsp lemon juice

1 clove garlic, crushed

3 tbsp olive oil

2 tbsp smooth peanut butter

salt and black pepper

1 To make the dressing, put the lemon juice, garlic, oil and peanut butter into a bowl, combine thoroughly and season.

2 Arrange the lettuce leaves, chicory and avocado in a large shallow dish. Pour over the dressing and sprinkle with spring onions and peanuts.

Note: Nutty tastes and textures work well with the avocados and bitter-leafed chicory in this salad. Serve as a starter with some chilled Chardonnay.

Serves 4   **Preparation** 15mins   **Cooking** 0   **Calories** 332   **Fat** 32g

sicilian

cauliflower salad

1 small cauliflower

30g/1oz seedless raisins

20g/²/₃oz toasted flaked almonds

2 tbsp chopped fresh flat-leaf parsley

For the dressing

grated rind and juice of 1 small lemon

$^1/_2$ tsp ground cinnamon

pinch of cayenne pepper

5 tbsp extra virgin olive oil

2 tsp balsamic vinegar

1 tsp superfine sugar

salt and black pepper

Serves *4* ***Preparation*** *15mins plus 1hr cooling and 10 mins soaking* ***Cooking*** *3mins* ***Calories*** *211* ***Fat*** *18g*

1 Cut the cauliflower into small florets and slice the stalk into bite-sized pieces. Cook in lightly salted, boiling water for 2-3 minutes, until softened but still firm to the bite. Drain well.

2 To make the dressing, place the lemon juice in a screw-top jar with the cinnamon, cayenne, oil, vinegar, sugar and seasoning and shake well, or place the ingredients in a bowl and mix with a fork. Pour the dressing over the cauliflower and toss to coat. Leave to cool for 1 hour.

3 Meanwhile, pour enough boiling water over the raisins to cover, then leave for 10 minutes to plump up. Drain and chop roughly. Scatter over the cauliflower with the almonds, lemon rind and parsley and toss lightly.

three bean

rice salad

1 Cook the rice according to the packet instructions and until tender. Meanwhile, cook the baby broad beans in a saucepan of boiling water for 4-5 minutes, until tender. Rinse under cold water and drain, then remove the skins if you want. Rinse the rice under cold water, drain and place in a salad bowl.

2 To make the dressing, place the tomato juice, olive oil, vinegar, mustard, garlic, coriander (cilantro) and black pepper in a small bowl and whisk together until thoroughly mixed.

3 Pour the dressing over the rice and stir to mix well. Add the broad beans, black-eye beans, kidney beans, pepper (capsicum) and spring onions and mix well. Cover and refrigerate before serving. Garnish with fresh coriander (cilantro).

Note: It's the tomato dressing which really makes this brown rice and bean salad taste so good. If you want to serve it warm, rinse the rice in boiling water before dressing it.

225g/8oz brown rice

170g/6oz frozen baby broad beans

400g/14oz can black-eye beans, drained and rinsed

200g/7oz can red kidney beans, drained and rinsed

1 red pepper (capsicum), deseeded and cut into pieces

1 bunch spring onions, chopped

fresh coriander (cilantro) to garnish

For the dressing

145mL/5fl oz tomato juice

1 tbsp olive oil

1 tbsp white wine vinegar

2 tsp Dijon mustard

1 clove garlic, crushed

2 tbsp chopped fresh coriander (cilantro)

black pepper

Serves 4   **Preparation** 15mins
Cooking 40mins   **Calories** 380mg   **Fat** 6g

courgette

rounds with red pepper puree

3 courgettes (zucchini), grated

salt

4 tbsp snipped fresh chives, extra to garnish

2 tbsp chopped fresh coriander (cilantro), plus extra leaves to garnish

$1/4$ tsp grated nutmeg

1 spring onion, finely chopped, to garnish

For the purée

3 tbsp olive oil

3 red peppers (capsicum), cored, deseeded and chopped

salt and black pepper

1 Sprinkle courgettes (zucchini) with salt, place in a colander, then set aside for 30 minutes to draw out the excess moisture. Rinse under cold running water, then squeeze dry and mix with the chives, coriander (cilantro) and nutmeg. Pack the mixture into 4 ramekins – it should half-fill them. Refrigerate for 1 hour, or overnight.

2 To make the purée, put the oil into a saucepan, then add the peppers (capsicum) and season. Cook, covered, over a low heat for 15 minutes. Leave to cool for a few minutes, then blend to a smooth purée in a food processor, or with a hand blender. Press the purée through a sieve to remove the skins.

3 To serve, turn each ramekin onto a plate, giving it a sharp shake to dislodge the courgette (zucchini) round, spoon around sauce. Garnish with chives, spring onion and coriander (cilantro).

Serves 4   *Preparation* 15mins plus 30mins standing and 1hr chilling
Cooking 15mins   *Calories* 168   *Fat* 12g

beetroot,

pear and bitter leaf salad

55g/2oz walnut pieces

200g/7oz mixed salad leaves, including radicchio and frisée

225g/8oz cooked beetroot in natural juices, sliced

2 pears, quartered, cored, sliced

40g/1½oz Parmesan

fresh chives to garnish

For the dressing

2 tbsp chopped fresh herbs, including basil, chives, mint and parsley

4 tbsp walnut oil

2 tbsp extra virgin olive oil

1 clove garlic, crushed

2 tsp red wine vinegar

1 tsp clear honey

salt and black pepper

1 Preheat the grill to high. To make the dressing, blend the herbs, walnut oil, olive oil, garlic, vinegar and honey until smooth in a food processor or with a hand blender. Season to taste.

2 Place the walnuts on a baking sheet and grill for 2-3 minutes, until golden, turning often. Arrange the leaves, beetroot and pear slices on serving plates. Scatter over the walnuts, then shave over thin slivers of Parmesan, using a vegetable peeler. Spoon the dressing over the salad and garnish with whole chives.

Serves 4   **Preparation** 15mins   **Cooking** 5mins   **Calories** 354   **Fat** 32g

tomato

& bread salad

1 Preheat the grill to high. Toss the bread in the oil to coat evenly and spread out on a baking sheet. Grill for 1-2 minutes, until golden, turning occasionally, then leave to cool for 10 minutes.

2 Meanwhile, make the dressing. Heat the oil in a small saucepan and fry the chilli, stirring, for 1 minute or until softened but not browned. Remove from the heat, leave to cool slightly, then add the pesto and vinegar. Whisk with a fork and season.

3 Mix the toasted bread with the tomatoes, onion, and feta. Scatter the basil over the salad. Spoon over the dressing and toss lightly to combine.

Note: Fresh chilli in the dressing gives this chunky tomato salad an unexpected kick and the croûtons add extra crunch. It goes down well with a glass of full-bodied Chianti.

Serves *4*
Preparation *15 mins
plus 10mins cooling*
Cooking *3 mins*
Calories *387*
Fat *25g*

1 French bread baton, cubed

2 tbsp olive oil

3 large tomatoes, cut into 2½cm/1½in chunks

1 small red onion, thinly sliced

100g/3½oz feta, crumbled

handful of fresh basil leaves, torn

For the dressing

3 tbsp olive oil

1 red chilli, deseeded and finely chopped

2 tbsp red pesto

2 tbsp red wine vinegar

salt and black pepper

with pesto dressing

warm
spinach salad

with walnuts

1 Heat the oil in a wok or large heavy-based frying pan. Add the tomatoes, spinach, onion, walnut pieces and salt to taste. Cook for 1 minute or until the spinach begins to wilt, tossing to combine.

2 Transfer the vegetables to a large salad bowl and sprinkle with the coriander (cilantro) to garnish. Serve straight away.

Note: There's something seductive about warm salads – their flavours seem more intense. In this easy salad, walnuts, spinach and sun-dried tomatoes create a magical result.

2 tbsp walnut oil

5 sun-dried tomatoes in oil, drained and chopped

225g/8oz baby spinach

1 red onion, sliced into thin rings

2 tbsp walnut pieces

salt

3 tbsp chopped fresh coriander (cilantro) to garnish

Serves *4* **Preparation** *5mins* **Cooking** *2mins*
Calories *166* **Fat** *15g*

| 170g/6oz bulgar wheat |
| 2 medium eggs |
| 1 red onion, finely chopped |
| 2 cloves garlic, finely chopped |
| 1 red and 1 yellow pepper (capsicum), cored, deseeded and finely chopped |
| 1 tbsp each chopped fresh parsley, chives and coriander (cilantro) |
| 3 tbsp chopped fresh mint |
| grated rind and juice of 1 lemon |
| grated rind and juice of 1 lime |
| 3 tbsp olive oil |
| salt and black pepper |

summer
tabbouleh

1 Prepare the bulgar wheat according to the packet instructions, until tender. Meanwhile, bring a saucepan of water to the boil. Add the eggs and boil for 10 minutes. Cool under cold running water, then remove the shells and mash the eggs.

2 Add the onion, garlic, peppers (capsicum), parsley, chives, coriander (cilantro), mint, lemon and lime rind and juice, and the oil to the bulgar wheat, then mix well. Season to taste before serving.

Note: This Middle Eastern dish goes with almost anything. It's particularly good at buffets or barbecues, and you can also serve it as a main course with a large salad.

Serves 4 **Preparation** 25mins **Cooking** 10mins **Calories** 220 **Fat** 15g

main
meals

aubergine
& tomato

1 Place the aubergine (eggplant) slices in layers in a colander, sprinkling salt over each layer. Set aside for 30 minutes. Rinse and pat dry with kitchen towels.

2 Preheat the oven to 200°C/400°F/Gas Mark 6. Heat 2 tablespoons of the oil in a frying pan, then fry the aubergine (eggplant) slices for 4-5 minutes, turning once, until softened and golden brown. Remove from the pan. Add another tablespoon of oil to the pan, then fry the onion and garlic for 3-4 minutes, until softened and lightly browned.

3 Arrange a layer of tomatoes, a layer of aubergines (eggplant) then a layer of onions in a shallow round ovenproof dish, 20cm/8in in diameter, seasoning each layer and sprinkling with thyme. Continue layering until all the vegetables are used, finishing with a layer of tomatoes. Drizzle over the remaining oil, then cook for 20 minutes. Sprinkle with Parmesan and cook for a further 5-10 minutes, until golden.

Ingredients
1 aubergine (eggplant), thinly sliced
salt and black pepper
4 tbsp olive oil
1 onion, thinly sliced
2 cloves garlic, finely chopped
6 plum tomatoes, thinly sliced
2 tbsp chopped fresh thyme
3 tbsp freshly grated Parmesan

Serves 4   **Preparation** 20 plus 30mins standing
Cooking 40mins   **Calories** 185   **Fat** 14g

bake

sweetcorn
& mushroom

roulade

1 Preheat the oven to 200°C/400°F/Gas Mark 6. To make the sauce, roast the pepper (capsicum) for 20 minutes. Cool for 10 minutes, then skin and chop. Cover the tomatoes with boiling water and leave for 30 seconds. Peel, deseed and chop, then combine with the pepper (capsicum), yoghurt, coriander (cilantro) and seasoning.

2 Melt 15g/½oz butter in a saucepan, then fry the mushrooms for 3-4 minutes. Add 15g/½oz flour, stir for 1 minute, then remove from the heat and gradually stir in the stock. Return to the heat and simmer, stirring, for 1-2 minutes, until thickened. Add the sweetcorn and keep warm. Grease a 25 x 30cm/10 x 12in Swiss roll tin and line with baking paper.

3 Melt the remaining butter in a pan and stir in the rest of the flour. Cook for 1 minute, then remove from the heat and slowly stir in the milk. Bring to the boil, stirring. Cool slightly, then beat in the egg yolks. Whisk the whites until stiff, then fold into the yolk mixture. Pour into the tin, then cook for 15 minutes or until golden. Turn out and peel off the lining. Spread over the filling, then roll up and serve with the sauce.

65g/2¼oz butter, plus extra for greasing

125g/4½oz mushrooms, chopped

65g/2¼oz plain flour

145mL/5fl oz vegetable stock

115g/4oz canned or frozen sweetcorn, drained or defrosted

170mL/6fl oz milk

4 medium eggs, separated

For the pepper sauce

1 red pepper (capsicum), deseeded and halved

2 tomatoes

155g/5½oz Greek yoghurt

1 tbsp chopped fresh coriander (cilantro)

salt and black pepper

Serves 4   **Preparation** 30mins plus 10mins cooling
Cooking 45mins   **Calories** 364   **Fat** 25g

harvest

vegetable bake

1 onion, sliced

2 leeks, sliced

2 sticks celery, chopped

2 carrots, thinly sliced

1 red pepper (capsicum), deseeded and sliced

510g/18oz mixed root vegetables, such as sweet potato, parsnip and turnip, cubed

170g/6oz mushrooms, sliced

400g/14oz can chopped tomatoes

6 tbsp dry cider

1 tsp dried thyme

1 tsp dried oregano

black pepper

fresh herbs, such as basil and coriander (cilantro), to garnish

1 Preheat the oven to 180°C/350°F/Gas Mark 4. Place the onion, leeks, celery, carrots, pepper (capsicum), cubed root vegetables and mushrooms in a large ovenproof casserole dish and mix well. Stir in the tomatoes, cider, thyme, oregano and black pepper.

2 Cover and bake in the centre of the oven for 1-1³/₄ hours, until the vegetables are cooked through and tender, stirring once or twice. Garnish with fresh herbs.

Serves 4   **Preparation** 10mins   **Cooking** 1hr 15mins   **Calories** 154   **Fat** 2g

stortelli

with mixed roasted vegetables

4 ripe tomatoes

1 small or ¹/₂ large aubergine (eggplant), thickly sliced

1 courgette (zucchini), thickly sliced

1 red or yellow pepper (capsicum), cut into quarters and deseeded

2 red onions, thickly sliced

salt and black pepper

5 tbsp extra virgin olive oil

2 garlic cloves, chopped

24 basil leaves, torn

340g/12oz dried pasta spirals (stortelli)

freshly grated Parmesan to serve

Serves *4* ***Preparation*** *20mins*
Cooking *50mins* ***Calories*** *543* ***Fat*** *20g*

1 Preheat the oven to 200°C/400°F/Gas Mark 6. Place the tomatoes in a bowl and pour over boiling water. Leave for 30 seconds, then peel, deseed and thickly slice.

2 Place the tomatoes, aubergine (eggplant), courgette (zucchini), pepper (capsicum) and onions in a shallow roasting tin. Season and drizzle with 2 tablespoons of the oil. Shake the tray gently to cover the vegetables with the oil. Bake for 40 minutes or until the vegetables are tender and slightly browned.

3 Mix together the remaining oil, garlic and basil. Cook the pasta in plenty of boiling salted water, until tender but still firm to the bite, then drain. Toss with the basil mixture, spoon onto 4 warmed plates and top with the roasted vegetables. Serve the Parmesan separately.

lasagne
with spinach,

1 Preheat the oven to 200°C/400°F/Gas Mark 6. Rinse the spinach and place in a saucepan with water still clinging to its leaves. Cover and cook for 5 minutes or until wilted. Drain, refresh under cold water and squeeze out all excess liquid. Chop finely. Cook the lasagne in plenty of boiling salted water, until tender but still firm to the bite, then drain and pat dry with kitchen towels.

2 Brush a 30 x 20cm/12 x 8in ovenproof dish with a little of the melted butter. In a bowl, combine the spinach, Fontina or Gruyère, Parmesan, ricotta, crème fraîche, nutmeg, salt and pepper.

3 Cover the base of the dish with a layer of lasagne sheets and spread over 3 tablespoons of the spinach mixture. Repeat the layering until all the lasagne is used, making no more than 6 layers. Finish with the remaining spinach mixture. Drizzle with the remaining melted butter, then cook for 20-30 minutes, until golden brown.

Serves *4*
Preparation *20mins*
Cooking *40mins*
Calories *596*
Fat *41g*

455g/16oz fresh spinach

170g/6oz dried lasagne

salt and black pepper

55g/2oz unsalted butter, melted

40g/1½oz Fontina or Gruyère, coarsely grated

40g/1½oz Parmesan, freshly grated

255g/9oz tub ricotta

160mL/5fl oz crème fraîche

freshly grated nutmeg

ricotta & fontina

bean,

lentil &

aubergine moussaka

1 Add the lentils to a saucepan of boiling water, cover and simmer for 30 minutes or until tender. Drain, rinse, then drain again and set aside.

2 Preheat the oven to 180°C/350°F/Gas Mark 4. Meanwhile, cook the aubergine (eggplant) slices in a saucepan of boiling water for 2 minutes. Drain, pat dry with kitchen towels and set aside.

3 Heat the oil in a frying pan, add the leeks, celery, garlic and pepper (capsicum) and cook for 5 minutes or until slightly softened. Add the cooked lentils, tomatoes, wine, tomato purée, beans, mixed herbs and black pepper. Cover and bring to the boil, then simmer for 10 minutes or until the vegetables have softened.

4 Spoon half the bean and lentil mixture into a shallow ovenproof dish and layer over half the aubergine (eggplant). Repeat. Mix together the yoghurt and eggs and pour over the top. Sprinkle over the Parmesan. Cook for 40 minutes or until golden brown and bubbling. Garnish with fresh herbs.

Serves 4   ***Preparation*** 30mins
Cooking 1hr 20mins
Calories 370   ***Fat*** 13g

85g/3oz continental lentils, rinsed and drained

1 aubergine (eggplant), thinly sliced

2 tbsp olive oil

2 leeks, sliced

2 sticks celery, chopped

2 cloves garlic, crushed

1 yellow pepper (capsicum), deseeded and diced

400g/14oz can chopped tomatoes

5 tbsp dry white wine

2 tbsp tomato purée

400g/14oz can black-eye beans, drained and rinsed

2 tsp dried mixed herbs

black pepper

300mL/10½fl oz low-fat natural yoghurt

2 medium eggs

25g/1oz Parmesan, finely grated

fresh herbs, such as basil, to garnish

moroccan

potato & lemon casserole

3 tbsp olive oil

2 onions, sliced

3 cloves garlic, chopped

2 red chillies, finely chopped

I tsp ground cumin

I tsp ground coriander (cilantro)

900g/2lb waxy potatoes, such as Charlotte, cut into 5mm/¼in thick slices

grated rind of I lemon, and juice of I or 2 lemons

900mL/32fl oz vegetable stock

salt and black pepper

4 tbsp soured cream to serve and 3 tbsp chopped fresh parsley to garnish

I Preheat the oven to 200°C/400°F/Gas Mark 6. Heat the oil in a flameproof and ovenproof casserole dish. Add the onions, garlic, chillies, cumin and coriander (cilantro), then gently fry for 1-2 minutes to release their flavours.

2 Stir in the potatoes, lemon rind and juice to taste, then add the stock and seasoning. Bring to the boil, cover, then cook in the oven for 40 minutes or until the vegetables are tender and the liquid has reduced slightly.

3 Transfer to plates and top each serving with a spoonful of soured cream. Sprinkle over fresh parsley to garnish.

Serves 4   *Preparation* 20mins   *Cooking* 45mins   *Calories* 386   *Fat* 16g

pasta

primavera

55g/2oz butter

225g/8oz baby spinach

510g/18oz fresh peas
(unshelled weight),
shelled

510g/18oz broad beans
(unshelled weight),
shelled

salt and black pepper

4 tbsp crème fraîche

1 bunch spring onions,
finely sliced

2 tbsp finely chopped
fresh parsley

85g/3oz Parmesan,
grated

340g/12oz dried penne
(pasta quills)

1 Melt the butter in a saucepan, add the spinach, cover, and cook for 5 minutes or until the leaves wilt. Set aside to cool. Cook the peas and beans in a little boiling salted water for 5 minutes or until tender, then drain.

2 Blend the spinach and crème fraîche to a purée in a food processor or with a hand blender. Return the purée to the pan and stir in the peas and beans. Mix in the spring onions and parsley, season and add half the Parmesan. Keep warm over a low heat.

3 Meanwhile, cook the pasta in boiling salted water according to the packet instructions, until tender but still firm to the bite. Drain, then toss with the spinach sauce. Serve with the remaining Parmesan.

Serves 4   **Preparation** 25mins   **Cooking** 20mins   **Calories** 612   **Fat** 25g

tortilla
with sweetcorn

& sun-dried tomatoes

225g/8oz potatoes,
thickly sliced

3 tbsp olive oil

3 tbsp canned
sweetcorn, drained

4 sun-dried tomatoes in
oil, drained and chopped

2 tbsp chopped fresh
parsley

6 medium eggs, beaten

salt and black pepper

1 Boil the potatoes for 10 minutes and leave to cool slightly. Heat the oil in a large, flameproof, heavy-based frying pan, add the potato and fry over a high heat for 2-3 minutes, until browned and crisp. Reduce the heat, then stir in the sweetcorn and tomatoes and heat through for 1-2 minutes.

2 Preheat the grill to medium. Add the parsley to the beaten eggs and season, then pour over the vegetables in the frying pan. Cook over a low heat for 3-4 minutes, until the omelette base is set and lightly browned.

3 Place the pan under the grill for 1-2 minutes, until the top is set and golden. Leave to cool slightly, then cut into 4 wedges and serve with salad.

Note: You can choose any combination of vegetables and herbs you like for this Spanish-style omelette, but make quite sure the potato is crisp and golden before pouring in the egg.

Serves 4   **Preparation** 15mins   **Cooking** 20mins
Calories 324   **Fat** 23g

spinach

souffle

455g/16oz fresh spinach

30g/1oz sunflower spread, plus extra for greasing

1 tbsp finely grated Parmesan

30g/1oz plain flour

255mL/9fl oz half-fat milk

4 medium eggs, separated, plus 1 extra egg white

100g/3½oz half-fat mature Cheddar, finely grated

black pepper

large pinch of ground nutmeg

1 Rinse the spinach, remove any coarse stalks or leaves and place in a large saucepan. Cover and cook over a low heat for 4-5 minutes or until it has wilted. Drain and squeeze out any excess water. Chop roughly and set aside.

2 Preheat the oven to 190°C/375°F/Gas Mark 5. Grease a 1½ litre/53fl oz, 18cm/7in soufflé dish, sprinkle with Parmesan and set aside. Gently heat the sunflower spread, flour and milk in a pan, whisking continuously, until the sauce boils. Simmer for 3 minutes, stirring. Transfer to a large bowl, add the spinach and mix well. Gradually beat in the egg yolks and 85g/3oz of the Cheddar, then season with pepper and nutmeg. Whisk the egg whites in a clean dry bowl until stiff (this is easiest with an electric whisk), then fold into the spinach mixture.

3 Spoon the mixture into the prepared dish and sprinkle with the remaining Cheddar. Bake for 30 minutes or until well risen and lightly set.

Serves 4
Preparation 3 mins
Cooking 40mins
Calories 284
Fat 18g

potato

cheese and onion pie

455g/16oz pack fresh shortcrust pastry

455g/16oz waxy potatoes, such as Charlotte, very thinly sliced

1 small onion, very thinly sliced

100g/3½oz hard tasty cheese finely grated

salt and black pepper

145mL/5oz carton double cream

Serves *4*   **Preparation** *30mins plus 10mins cooling*   **Cooking** *1hr 15mins*   **Calories** *910*   **Fat** *62g*

1 Preheat the oven to 180°C/350°F/Gas Mark 4. Roll out two-thirds of the pastry on a lightly floured work surface and use it to line a 23cm/9in flan dish. Arrange the potatoes in a single layer over the base of the dish, then top with a layer each of the onion and cheese, seasoning well between each layer. Pour over the cream.

2 Roll out the remaining pastry to make a lid. Lightly dampen the edges of the pie with water. Place the pastry lid on top and pinch the edges together to seal well.

3 Bake for 1-1¾ hours, until the potatoes and onions are tender. Leave for 10 minutes before serving to allow the cheese to cool slightly.

root vegetable curry

1 Heat the oil in a large saucepan. Add the onion, chilli, garlic and ginger and cook for 5 minutes or until softened, stirring occasionally. Stir in the flour, coriander (cilantro), cumin and turmeric and cook gently, stirring, for 1 minute to release the flavours.

2 Gradually stir in the stock, then add the passata, cubed root vegetables and the carrots, season with black pepper and mix well.

3 Bring to the boil, stirring, then cover, reduce the heat and simmer for 45 minutes or until the vegetables are tender, stirring occasionally. Garnish with fresh coriander (cilantro).

Note: This spicy root vegetable curry is based on a traditional Moroccan dish. So, as a change from boiled rice, try serving it with some hot fluffy couscous instead.

1 tbsp olive oil
1 onion, chopped
1 green chilli, deseeded and finely chopped
1 clove garlic, finely chopped
2½cm/1in piece fresh root ginger, finely chopped
2 tbsp plain flour
2 tsp each ground coriander (cilantro), ground cumin and turmeric
285mL/10fl oz vegetable stock
200mL/7fl oz passata
750g/26oz mixed root vegetables, such as potato, sweet potato, celeriac and swede, cubed
2 carrots, thinly sliced
black pepper
chopped fresh coriander (cilantro) to garnish

Serves 4   **Preparation** 20mins   **Cooking** 55mins   **Calories** 219   **Fat** 4g

weights and measures

quick converter

Metric	Imperial
5mm	$^1/_4$ in
1cm	$^1/_2$ in
2cm	$^3/_4$ in
2$^1/_2$cm	1 in
5cm	2 in
10$^1/_2$cm	4 in
15cm	6 in
20cm	8 in
23cm	9 in
25cm	10 in
30cm	12 in

metric cups and spoons

Metric	Cups	Imperial
60mL	$^1/_4$ cup	2 fl oz
80mL	$^1/_3$ cup	2$^1/_2$ fl oz
125mL	$^1/_2$ cup	4 fl oz
250mL	1 cup	8 fl oz
Metric	**Spoons**	
1$^1/_4$mL	$^1/_4$ teaspoon	
2$^1/_2$mL	$^1/_2$ teaspoon	
5mL	1 teaspoon	
20mL	1 tablespoon	

measuring liquids

Metric	Imperial	Cups
30mL	1 fl oz	
55mL	2 fl oz	$^1/_4$ cup
85mL	3 fl oz	
115mL	4 fl oz	$^1/_2$ cup
150mL	5$^1/_4$ fl oz	
170mL	6 fl oz	$^2/_3$ cup
185mL	6$^1/_2$ fl oz	
200mL	7 fl oz	
225mL	8 fl oz	1 cup
285mL	10 fl oz	
370mL	13 fl oz	
400mL	14 fl oz	
455mL	16 fl oz	2 cups
570mL	20 fl oz	
1 litre	35.3 fl oz	4 cups

oven temperatures

°C	°F	Gas Mark
120	250	$^1/_4$
140	275	1
150	300	2
160	326	3
180	350	4
190	375	5
200	400	6
220	425	7
240	475	8
250	500	9

measuring dry ingredients

Metric	Imperial
15g	$^1/_2$oz
20g	$^2/_3$oz
30g	1oz
55g	2oz
85g	3oz
115g	4oz
125g	$4^1/_2$oz
140g	5oz
170g	6oz
200g	7oz
225g	8oz ($^1/_2$lb)
255g	9oz
315g	11oz
370g	13oz
400g	14oz
425g	15oz
455g	16oz(1lb)
680g	1 lb 8oz
1kg	2.2lb
$1^1/_2$ kg	3.3lb

chicken types

Type	Age	Size
Poussin	under 6 weeks	1lb
Rock Cornish game hen	4-5 weeks	$1-1^1/_2$ lb
Broiler	7-9 weeks	$1^1/_2$-2 lb
Fryer	9-12 weeks	3-4lb
Roaster	10-12 weeks	over 5lb
Capon	16-20 weeks	6-9 lb
Stewing	under 10 months	4-6 lb

index